Welcome to your Boutique Planner!

The Online Boutique Planner

Printed in the United States of America
First Printing: January 2018
Rich Girl Collective, LLC

ISBN-13: 978-1979388085

Dedication

This book was created for all current and future boutique owners. Over the past couple of years, I've run 3 successful online boutiques and one of the main keys to my success was planning. This planner will help you plan out your goals, stay organized, and keep track of your vendors, sales and everything need to run a profitable boutique.

To my parents and my amazing husband who have always believed in me and supported all of my dreams: I couldn't have done it without you. Love Ya'll!

This Planner Belongs to:

Jonellen Harris

Reflectionz Boutique

Goal of this Planner

This book was created for current and future boutique owners. Over the past couple of years, I've run 3 successful online boutiques and one of the main keys to my success was planning. This planner will help you plan out your goals, stay organized, and keep track of your vendors, sales and everything need to run a profitable boutique.

How to Use This Planner

Keep all of your boutique business in this one planner. It makes it much easier to have everything in one place. It reduces stress because it keeps you more organized.

Review your goals, monthly, weekly and daily to make sure you are staying on track and hitting your sales goals.

Use the notes section at the end of the planner to list any ideas that you may come up with.

I suggest you write in your planner with a pencil, just in case you have to go back and update your goals and make changes. Use a highlighter to highlight important things.

Most importantly, have fun! Running a boutique can be a bit stressful at times but it can also be very rewarding.

My Boutique's Core

_____

NAME:	TAGLINE:

UNIQUE SELLING PROPOSITION

....

....

....

MISSION STATEMENT
What is your boutique about + who is it for?

MY STRENGTHS	CORE VALUES
....	1.
....	2.
....	3.
....	4.
	5.

PRODUCTS

My Boutique's Core
Cont.

PARTNERS	RESOURCES

Featured Products

1.	2.	3.	4.

BRAINSTORM ANNOUNCEMENTS + PROMOTIONS

ABOUT

VENDORS:

My Boutique's Core

NAME:

TAGLINE:

UNIQUE SELLING PROPOSITION

MISSION STATEMENT
What is your boutique about + who is it for?

MY STRENGTHS	CORE VALUES
	1.
	2.
	3.
	4.
	5.

PRODUCTS

My Boutique's Core
Cont.

PARTNERS	RESOURCES

Featured Products

1.	2.	3.	4.

BRAINSTORM ANNOUNCEMENTS + PROMOTIONS

ABOUT

VENDORS:

My Boutique's Core

NAME:	TAGLINE:

UNIQUE SELLING PROPOSITION

MISSION STATEMENT
What is your boutique about + who is it for?

MY STRENGTHS	CORE VALUES
	1.
	2.
	3.
	4.
	5.

PRODUCTS

My Boutique's Core
Cont.

PARTNERS	RESOURCES

Featured Products

1.	2.	3.	4.

BRAINSTORM ANNOUNCEMENTS + PROMOTIONS

ABOUT

VENDORS:

Ideal Customer
Profile

	NAME:

	AGE:	GENDER:
IF IT'S HELPFUL, ATTACH A PHOTO OF YOUR IDEAL CUSTOMER	LOCATION:	
	VOCATION:	
	FAMILY:	
	PERSONALITY:	

WHERE DO THEY SHOP?	WHAT DO THEY READ/WATCH?	WHAT DO THEY WEAR?

WHAT DO THEY EAT?	WHAT DO THEY LISTEN?	WHAT DO THEY ENJOY?

FAVORITE WEBSITES	CURRENT GOALS
	1.
	2.
	3.
	4.

Ideal Customer
Profile

	NAME:

IF IT'S HELPFUL,
ATTACH A PHOTO
OF YOUR IDEAL CUSTOMER

AGE: **GENDER:**

LOCATION:

VOCATION:

FAMILY:

PERSONALITY:

WHERE DO THEY SHOP?	WHAT DO THEY READ/WATCH?	WHAT DO THEY WEAR?

WHAT DO THEY EAT?	WHAT DO THEY LISTEN?	WHAT DO THEY ENJOY?

FAVORITE WEBSITES	CURRENT GOALS
	1.
	2.
	3.
	4.

Ideal Customer
Profile

IF IT'S HELPFUL,
ATTACH A PHOTO
OF YOUR IDEAL CUSTOMER

NAME:

AGE: GENDER:

LOCATION:

VOCATION:

FAMILY:

PERSONALITY:

WHERE DO THEY SHOP?	WHAT DO THEY READ/WATCH?	WHAT DO THEY WEAR?

WHAT DO THEY EAT?	WHAT DO THEY LISTEN?	WHAT DO THEY ENJOY?

FAVORITE WEBSITES	CURRENT GOALS
	1.
	2.
	3.
	4.

My Boutique's Style

GENERAL AESTHETIC

KEYWORDS:	SKETCHES + DOODLES
....	
....	
....	
....	
....	

COLOR PALETTE

MAIN	SECONDARY 1	SECONDARY 2	COMPLEMENTARY 1	COMPLEMENTARY 2
HEX	HEX	HEX	HEX	HEX ....
CMYK	CMYK	CMYK	CMYK	CMYK ......
RGB	RGB	RGB	RGB	RGB ....

PATTERNS + TEXTURES

TYPOGRAPHY

My Boutique's Policies

PAYMENT OPTIONS:

☐ PAYPAL   ☐ VISA/MASTERCARD   ☐ OTHER: ....

SHIPPING METHODS

RETURNS + EXCHANGES:

OTHER INFO:

Year in a Glance
+ Important Dates

	JANUARY	FEBRUARY	MARCH
Quarter 1			

	APRIL	MAY	JUNE
Quarter 2			

	JULY	AUGUST	SEPTEMBER
Quarter 3			

	OCTOBER	NOVEMBER	DECEMBER
Quarter 4			

Year in a Glance

+ Important Dates

	JANUARY	FEBRUARY	MARCH
Quarter 1			

	APRIL	MAY	JUNE
Quarter 2			

	JULY	AUGUST	SEPTEMBER
Quarter 3			

	OCTOBER	NOVEMBER	DECEMBER
Quarter 4			

Year in a Glance
+ Important Dates

	JANUARY	FEBRUARY	MARCH
Quarter 1			

	APRIL	MAY	JUNE
Quarter 2			

	JULY	AUGUST	SEPTEMBER
Quarter 3			

	OCTOBER	NOVEMBER	DECEMBER
Quarter 4			

Monthly Goals
Planner

MONTH:	MAIN BUSINESS GOAL:

Break down your main goal into steps you can do each week:

	NOTES:
WEEK 1	
WEEK 2	
WEEK 3	
WEEK 4	
WEEK 5	

Monthly Goals
Planner

MONTH:	MAIN BUSINESS GOAL:

Break down your main goal into steps you can do each week:

NOTES:

WEEK 1	
WEEK 2	
WEEK 3	
WEEK 4	
WEEK 5	

Monthly Goals
Planner

MONTH:	MAIN BUSINESS GOAL:

Break down your main goal into steps you can do each week:

NOTES:

WEEK 1

WEEK 2

WEEK 3

WEEK 4

WEEK 5

Monthly Goals
Planner

_____

MONTH:	MAIN BUSINESS GOAL:

Break down your main goal into steps you can do each week:

NOTES:

WEEK 1

WEEK 2

WEEK 3

WEEK 4

WEEK 5

Monthly Goals
Planner

MONTH:	MAIN BUSINESS GOAL:

Break down your main goal into steps you can do each week:

NOTES:

WEEK 1

WEEK 2

WEEK 3

WEEK 4

WEEK 5

Monthly Goals
Planner

MONTH:	MAIN BUSINESS GOAL:

Break down your main goal into steps you can do each week:

NOTES:

WEEK 1

WEEK 2

WEEK 3

WEEK 4

WEEK 5

Monthly Goals
Planner

MONTH:	MAIN BUSINESS GOAL:

Break down your main goal into steps you can do each week:

NOTES:

WEEK 1

WEEK 2

WEEK 3

WEEK 4

WEEK 5

Monthly Goals
Planner

MONTH:	MAIN BUSINESS GOAL:

Break down your main goal into steps you can do each week:

NOTES:

WEEK 1

WEEK 2

WEEK 3

WEEK 4

WEEK 5

Monthly Goals
Planner

MONTH:	MAIN BUSINESS GOAL:

Break down your main goal into steps you can do each week:

		NOTES:
WEEK 1		
WEEK 2		
WEEK 3		
WEEK 4		
WEEK 5		

Monthly Goals
Planner

MONTH:	MAIN BUSINESS GOAL:

Break down your main goal into steps you can do each week: NOTES:

WEEK 1

WEEK 2

WEEK 3

WEEK 4

WEEK 5

Monthly Goals
Planner

MONTH:	MAIN BUSINESS GOAL:

Break down your main goal into steps you can do each week: NOTES:

WEEK 1

WEEK 2

WEEK 3

WEEK 4

WEEK 5

Monthly Goals
Planner

MONTH:	MAIN BUSINESS GOAL:

Break down your main goal into steps you can do each week:　NOTES:

WEEK 1

WEEK 2

WEEK 3

WEEK 4

WEEK 5

Goals Tracker

GOAL:	REWARD:	DUE DATE: ☐

WHAT OBSTACLES COULD YOU FACE + HOW WILL YOU OVERCOME THEM?	KEY TOOLS + RESOURCES
	☐
	☐
	☐
	☐
	☐

ACTION STEPS + TASKS	DEADLINE	MILESTONES + REWARDS
☐		
☐		
☐		
☐		
☐		
☐		
☐		
☐		
☐		
☐		
☐		
☐		
☐		
☐		

Goals Tracker

GOAL:	REWARD:	DUE DATE: ☐

WHAT OBSTACLES COULD YOU FACE + HOW WILL YOU OVERCOME THEM?	KEY TOOLS + RESOURCES
	☐
	☐
	☐
	☐
	☐

ACTION STEPS + TASKS	DEADLINE	MILESTONES + REWARDS
☐		
☐		
☐		
☐		
☐		
☐		
☐		
☐		
☐		
☐		
☐		
☐		
☐		
☐		

Goals Tracker

GOAL:	REWARD:	DUE DATE: ☐

WHAT OBSTACLES COULD YOU FACE + HOW WILL YOU OVERCOME THEM?	KEY TOOLS + RESOURCES
	☐
	☐
	☐
	☐
	☐

ACTION STEPS + TASKS	DEADLINE	MILESTONES + REWARDS
☐		
☐		
☐		
☐		
☐		
☐		
☐		
☐		
☐		
☐		
☐		
☐		
☐		
☐		

Goals Tracker

GOAL:	REWARD:	DUE DATE: ☐

WHAT OBSTACLES COULD YOU FACE + HOW WILL YOU OVERCOME THEM?	KEY TOOLS + RESOURCES
	☐
	☐
	☐
	☐
	☐

ACTION STEPS + TASKS	DEADLINE	MILESTONES + REWARDS
☐		
☐		
☐		
☐		
☐		
☐		
☐		
☐		
☐		
☐		
☐		
☐		
☐		
☐		
☐		

Goals Tracker

GOAL:	REWARD:	DUE DATE: ☐

WHAT OBSTACLES COULD YOU FACE + HOW WILL YOU OVERCOME THEM?

....

....

....

....

....

KEY TOOLS + RESOURCES

☐ ....

☐ ....

☐ ....

☐ ....

☐ ....

ACTION STEPS + TASKS	DEADLINE
☐	
☐	
☐	
☐	
☐	
☐	
☐	
☐	
☐	
☐	
☐	
☐	
☐	
☐	
☐	

MILESTONES + REWARDS

Goals Tracker

GOAL:	REWARD:	DUE DATE: ☐

WHAT OBSTACLES COULD YOU FACE + HOW WILL YOU OVERCOME THEM?	KEY TOOLS + RESOURCES
	☐
	☐
	☐
	☐
	☐

ACTION STEPS + TASKS	DEADLINE	MILESTONES + REWARDS
☐		
☐		
☐		
☐		
☐		
☐		
☐		
☐		
☐		
☐		
☐		
☐		
☐		
☐		
☐		

Goals Tracker

GOAL:	REWARD:	DUE DATE: ☐

WHAT OBSTACLES COULD YOU FACE + HOW WILL YOU OVERCOME THEM?	KEY TOOLS + RESOURCES
	☐
	☐
	☐
	☐
	☐

ACTION STEPS + TASKS	DEADLINE	MILESTONES + REWARDS
☐		
☐		
☐		
☐		
☐		
☐		
☐		
☐		
☐		
☐		
☐		
☐		
☐		
☐		
☐		

Goals Tracker

| GOAL: | REWARD: | DUE DATE: ☐ |

WHAT OBSTACLES COULD YOU FACE + HOW WILL YOU OVERCOME THEM?

KEY TOOLS + RESOURCES

☐

☐

☐

☐

☐

ACTION STEPS + TASKS	DEADLINE	MILESTONES + REWARDS
☐		
☐		
☐		
☐		
☐		
☐		
☐		
☐		
☐		
☐		
☐		
☐		
☐		
☐		
☐		

Goals Tracker

GOAL:	REWARD:	DUE DATE: ☐

WHAT OBSTACLES COULD YOU FACE + HOW WILL YOU OVERCOME THEM?	KEY TOOLS + RESOURCES
	☐
	☐
	☐
	☐
	☐

ACTION STEPS + TASKS	DEADLINE	MILESTONES + REWARDS
☐		
☐		
☐		
☐		
☐		
☐		
☐		
☐		
☐		
☐		
☐		
☐		
☐		
☐		

Goals Tracker

GOAL:	REWARD:	DUE DATE: ☐

WHAT OBSTACLES COULD YOU FACE + HOW WILL YOU OVERCOME THEM?	KEY TOOLS + RESOURCES
	☐
	☐
	☐
	☐
	☐

ACTION STEPS + TASKS	DEADLINE	MILESTONES + REWARDS
☐		
☐		
☐		
☐		
☐		
☐		
☐		
☐		
☐		
☐		
☐		
☐		
☐		
☐		

New Product

PRODUCT:

| CATEGORY: | QUANTITY: | WHOLESALE PRICE: |
| OCASSION: | STYLE: | RETAIL PRICE: |

DESCRIPTION:

VARIATIONS:

MATERIALS

SHIPPING / DELIVERY:

IMAGE:

MARKETING IDEAS:

NOTES:

New Product

PRODUCT:

CATEGORY:

QUANTITY:

WHOLESALE PRICE:

OCASSION:

STYLE:

RETAIL PRICE:

DESCRIPTION:

VARIATIONS:

MATERIALS

SHIPPING / DELIVERY:

IMAGE:

MARKETING IDEAS:

NOTES:

New Product

PRODUCT:

| CATEGORY: | QUANTITY: | WHOLESALE PRICE: |
| OCASSION: | STYLE: | RETAIL PRICE: |

DESCRIPTION:

VARIATIONS:

MATERIALS

SHIPPING / DELIVERY:

IMAGE:

MARKETING IDEAS:

NOTES:

New Product

PRODUCT:

CATEGORY:

QUANTITY:

WHOLESALE PRICE:

OCASSION:

STYLE:

RETAIL PRICE:

DESCRIPTION:

VARIATIONS:

MATERIALS

SHIPPING / DELIVERY:

IMAGE:

MARKETING IDEAS:

NOTES:

New Product

PRODUCT:

CATEGORY: QUANTITY: WHOLESALE PRICE:

OCASSION: STYLE: RETAIL PRICE:

DESCRIPTION:

VARIATIONS:

MATERIALS

SHIPPING / DELIVERY:

IMAGE:

MARKETING IDEAS:

NOTES:

New Product

PRODUCT:

| CATEGORY: | QUANTITY: | WHOLESALE PRICE: |
| OCASSION: | STYLE: | RETAIL PRICE: |

DESCRIPTION:

VARIATIONS:

MATERIALS

SHIPPING / DELIVERY:

IMAGE:

MARKETING IDEAS:

NOTES:

_____ *New Product*

PRODUCT:

| CATEGORY: | QUANTITY: | WHOLESALE PRICE: |
| OCASSION: | STYLE: | RETAIL PRICE: |

DESCRIPTION:

VARIATIONS:

MATERIALS

SHIPPING / DELIVERY:

IMAGE:

MARKETING IDEAS:

NOTES:

New Product

PRODUCT:

| CATEGORY: | QUANTITY: | WHOLESALE PRICE: |
| OCASSION: | STYLE: | RETAIL PRICE: |

DESCRIPTION:

VARIATIONS:

MATERIALS

SHIPPING / DELIVERY:

IMAGE:

MARKETING IDEAS:

NOTES:

New Product

PRODUCT:

CATEGORY:

QUANTITY:

WHOLESALE PRICE:

OCASSION:

STYLE:

RETAIL PRICE:

DESCRIPTION:

VARIATIONS:

MATERIALS

SHIPPING / DELIVERY:

IMAGE:

MARKETING IDEAS:

NOTES:

New Product

PRODUCT:

CATEGORY:

QUANTITY:

WHOLESALE PRICE:

OCASSION:

STYLE:

RETAIL PRICE:

DESCRIPTION:

VARIATIONS:

MATERIALS

SHIPPING / DELIVERY:

IMAGE:

MARKETING IDEAS:

NOTES:

Pricing Products
Worksheet

ITEM	HARD COST	SHIPPING + HANDLING	TAXES	PROFIT %	TOTAL

Pricing Products
Worksheet

ITEM	HARD COST	SHIPPING + HANDLING	TAXES	PROFIT %	TOTAL

Pricing Products
Worksheet

ITEM	HARD COST	SHIPPING + HANDLING	TAXES	PROFIT %	TOTAL

Pricing Products
Worksheet

ITEM	HARD COST	SHIPPING + HANDLING	TAXES	PROFIT %	TOTAL

Pricing Products
Worksheet

ITEM	HARD COST	SHIPPING + HANDLING	TAXES	PROFIT %	TOTAL

Products Tracker

ITEM	PRODUCT NO	AVAILABLE SINCE	PRICE	OUT OF STOCK
				☐
				☐
				☐
				☐
				☐
				☐
				☐
				☐
				☐
				☐
				☐
				☐
				☐
				☐
				☐

Products Tracker

ITEM	PRODUCT NO	AVAILABLE SINCE	PRICE	OUT OF STOCK
				☐
				☐
				☐
				☐
				☐
				☐
				☐
				☐
				☐
				☐
				☐
				☐
				☐
				☐
				☐

Products Tracker

ITEM	PRODUCT NO	AVAILABLE SINCE	PRICE	OUT OF STOCK
				☐
				☐
				☐
				☐
				☐
				☐
				☐
				☐
				☐
				☐
				☐
				☐
				☐
				☐
				☐

Products Tracker

ITEM	PRODUCT NO	AVAILABLE SINCE	PRICE	OUT OF STOCK
				☐
				☐
				☐
				☐
				☐
				☐
				☐
				☐
				☐
				☐
				☐
				☐
				☐
				☐
				☐

Products Tracker

ITEM	PRODUCT NO	AVAILABLE SINCE	PRICE	OUT OF STOCK
				☐
				☐
				☐
				☐
				☐
				☐
				☐
				☐
				☐
				☐
				☐
				☐
				☐
				☐
				☐

Daily Sales
Tracker

DATE	DESCRIPTION	ORDER NO.	TOTAL
		TOTAL:	

Daily Sales
Tracker

DATE	DESCRIPTION	ORDER NO.	TOTAL
		TOTAL:	

Daily Sales
Tracker

DATE	DESCRIPTION	ORDER NO.	TOTAL
		TOTAL:	

Daily Sales
Tracker

DATE	DESCRIPTION	ORDER NO.	TOTAL
		TOTAL:	

Daily Sales
Tracker

DATE	DESCRIPTION	ORDER NO.	TOTAL
		TOTAL:	

Current Orders
Tracker

DATE	CUSTOMER	ORDER DETAILS	DEADLINE	SHIPPING DATE + TRACKING NO.	RECEIVED	REVIEWED
			☐		☐	☐
			☐		☐	☐
			☐		☐	☐
			☐		☐	☐
			☐		☐	☐
			☐		☐	☐
			☐		☐	☐
			☐		☐	☐
			☐		☐	☐
			☐		☐	☐
			☐		☐	☐
			☐		☐	☐
			☐		☐	☐
			☐		☐	☐

Current Orders
Tracker

DATE	CUSTOMER	ORDER DETAILS	DEADLINE	SHIPPING DATE + TRACKING NO.	RECEIVED	REVIEWED
			☐		☐	☐
			☐		☐	☐
			☐		☐	☐
			☐		☐	☐
			☐		☐	☐
			☐		☐	☐
			☐		☐	☐
			☐		☐	☐
			☐		☐	☐
			☐		☐	☐
			☐		☐	☐
			☐		☐	☐
			☐		☐	☐
			☐		☐	☐

Current Orders
Tracker

DATE	CUSTOMER	ORDER DETAILS	DEADLINE	SHIPPING DATE + TRACKING NO.	RECEIVED	REVIEWED
			☐		☐	☐
			☐		☐	☐
			☐		☐	☐
			☐		☐	☐
			☐		☐	☐
			☐		☐	☐
			☐		☐	☐
			☐		☐	☐
			☐		☐	☐
			☐		☐	☐
			☐		☐	☐
			☐		☐	☐
			☐		☐	☐
			☐		☐	☐

Current Orders
Tracker

DATE	CUSTOMER	ORDER DETAILS	DEADLINE	SHIPPING DATE + TRACKING NO.	RECEIVED	REVIEWED
			☐		☐	☐
			☐		☐	☐
			☐		☐	☐
			☐		☐	☐
			☐		☐	☐
			☐		☐	☐
			☐		☐	☐
			☐		☐	☐
			☐		☐	☐
			☐		☐	☐
			☐		☐	☐
			☐		☐	☐
			☐		☐	☐

69

Current Orders
Tracker

DATE	CUSTOMER	ORDER DETAILS	DEADLINE	SHIPPING DATE + TRACKING NO.	RECEIVED	REVIEWED
			☐		☐	☐
			☐		☐	☐
			☐		☐	☐
			☐		☐	☐
			☐		☐	☐
			☐		☐	☐
			☐		☐	☐
			☐		☐	☐
			☐		☐	☐
			☐		☐	☐
			☐		☐	☐
			☐		☐	☐
			☐		☐	☐
			☐		☐	☐

Current Orders
Tracker

DATE	CUSTOMER	ORDER DETAILS	DEADLINE	SHIPPING DATE + TRACKING NO.	RECEIVED	REVIEWED
			☐		☐	☐
			☐		☐	☐
			☐		☐	☐
			☐		☐	☐
			☐		☐	☐
			☐		☐	☐
			☐		☐	☐
			☐		☐	☐
			☐		☐	☐
			☐		☐	☐
			☐		☐	☐
			☐		☐	☐
			☐		☐	☐
			☐		☐	☐

71

Current Orders
Tracker

DATE	CUSTOMER	ORDER DETAILS	DEADLINE	SHIPPING DATE + TRACKING NO.	RECEIVED	REVIEWED
				☐	☐	☐
				☐	☐	☐
				☐	☐	☐
				☐	☐	☐
				☐	☐	☐
				☐	☐	☐
				☐	☐	☐
				☐	☐	☐
				☐	☐	☐
				☐	☐	☐
				☐	☐	☐
				☐	☐	☐
				☐	☐	☐

Current Orders
Tracker

DATE	CUSTOMER	ORDER DETAILS	DEADLINE	SHIPPING DATE + TRACKING NO.	RECEIVED	REVIEWED
			☐		☐	☐
			☐		☐	☐
			☐		☐	☐
			☐		☐	☐
			☐		☐	☐
			☐		☐	☐
			☐		☐	☐
			☐		☐	☐
			☐		☐	☐
			☐		☐	☐
			☐		☐	☐
			☐		☐	☐
			☐		☐	☐
			☐		☐	☐

Current Orders
Tracker

DATE	CUSTOMER	ORDER DETAILS	DEADLINE	SHIPPING DATE + TRACKING NO.	RECEIVED	REVIEWED
			☐		☐	☐
			☐		☐	☐
			☐		☐	☐
			☐		☐	☐
			☐		☐	☐
			☐		☐	☐
			☐		☐	☐
			☐		☐	☐
			☐		☐	☐
			☐		☐	☐
			☐		☐	☐
			☐			☐
			☐		☐	☐
			☐		☐	☐

Current Orders
Tracker

DATE	CUSTOMER	ORDER DETAILS	DEADLINE	SHIPPING DATE + TRACKING NO.	RECEIVED	REVIEWED
			☐		☐	☐
			☐		☐	☐
			☐		☐	☐
			☐		☐	☐
			☐		☐	☐
			☐		☐	☐
			☐		☐	☐
			☐		☐	☐
			☐		☐	☐
			☐		☐	☐
			☐		☐	☐
			☐		☐	☐
			☐		☐	☐
			☐		☐	☐

Returned Products

RETURNED ITEM: **TRACKING CODE:**

CUSTOMER:

REASON:

RECEIVED + DATE: ☐   AMOUNT REFUNDED: ☐

EXCHANGED FOR: ☐

RETURNED ITEM: **TRACKING CODE:**

CUSTOMER:

REASON:

RECEIVED + DATE: ☐   AMOUNT REFUNDED: ☐

EXCHANGED FOR: ☐

RETURNED ITEM: **TRACKING CODE:**

CUSTOMER:

REASON:

RECEIVED + DATE: ☐   AMOUNT REFUNDED: ☐

EXCHANGED FOR: ☐

RETURNED ITEM: **TRACKING CODE:**

CUSTOMER:

REASON:

RECEIVED + DATE: ☐   AMOUNT REFUNDED: ☐

EXCHANGED FOR: ☐

Returned Products

RETURNED ITEM:	TRACKING CODE:

CUSTOMER:

REASON:

RECEIVED + DATE: ☐   AMOUNT REFUNDED: ☐

EXCHANGED FOR: ☐

RETURNED ITEM:	TRACKING CODE:

CUSTOMER:

REASON:

RECEIVED + DATE: ☐   AMOUNT REFUNDED: ☐

EXCHANGED FOR: ☐

RETURNED ITEM:	TRACKING CODE:

CUSTOMER:

REASON:

RECEIVED + DATE: ☐   AMOUNT REFUNDED: ☐

EXCHANGED FOR: ☐

RETURNED ITEM:	TRACKING CODE:

CUSTOMER:

REASON:

RECEIVED + DATE: ☐   AMOUNT REFUNDED: ☐

EXCHANGED FOR: ☐

Returned Products

RETURNED ITEM:	TRACKING CODE:

CUSTOMER:

REASON:

RECEIVED + DATE: ☐   AMOUNT REFUNDED: ☐

EXCHANGED FOR: ☐

RETURNED ITEM:	TRACKING CODE:

CUSTOMER:

REASON:

RECEIVED + DATE: ☐   AMOUNT REFUNDED: ☐

EXCHANGED FOR: ☐

RETURNED ITEM:	TRACKING CODE:

CUSTOMER:

REASON:

RECEIVED + DATE: ☐   AMOUNT REFUNDED: ☐

EXCHANGED FOR: ☐

RETURNED ITEM:	TRACKING CODE:

CUSTOMER:

REASON:

RECEIVED + DATE: ☐   AMOUNT REFUNDED: ☐

EXCHANGED FOR: ☐

Returned Products

RETURNED ITEM:	TRACKING CODE:

CUSTOMER:

REASON:

RECEIVED + DATE: ☐   AMOUNT REFUNDED: ☐

EXCHANGED FOR: ☐

RETURNED ITEM:	TRACKING CODE:

CUSTOMER:

REASON:

RECEIVED + DATE: ☐   AMOUNT REFUNDED: ☐

EXCHANGED FOR: ☐

RETURNED ITEM:	TRACKING CODE:

CUSTOMER:

REASON:

RECEIVED + DATE: ☐   AMOUNT REFUNDED: ☐

EXCHANGED FOR: ☐

RETURNED ITEM:	TRACKING CODE:

CUSTOMER:

REASON:

RECEIVED + DATE: ☐   AMOUNT REFUNDED: ☐

EXCHANGED FOR: ☐

Returned Products

RETURNED ITEM:	TRACKING CODE:

CUSTOMER:

REASON:

RECEIVED + DATE: ☐   AMOUNT REFUNDED: ☐

EXCHANGED FOR: ☐

RETURNED ITEM:	TRACKING CODE:

CUSTOMER:

REASON:

RECEIVED + DATE: ☐   AMOUNT REFUNDED: ☐

EXCHANGED FOR: ☐

RETURNED ITEM:	TRACKING CODE:

CUSTOMER:

REASON:

RECEIVED + DATE: ☐   AMOUNT REFUNDED: ☐

EXCHANGED FOR: ☐

RETURNED ITEM:	TRACKING CODE:

CUSTOMER:

REASON:

RECEIVED + DATE: ☐   AMOUNT REFUNDED: ☐

EXCHANGED FOR: ☐

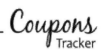

Coupons Tracker

COUPON	SALE	START DATE	END DATE

Discounts + Sales
Tracker

SALE / OCCASION	DISCOUNT	START DATE	END DATE

Products
Inventory

YEAR:	DATE:					
DESCRIPTION	QTY	QTY	QTY	QTY	QTY	QTY

Products
Inventory

YEAR:	DATE:					
DESCRIPTION	QTY	QTY	QTY	QTY	QTY	QTY

Products
Inventory

YEAR:	DATE:					
DESCRIPTION	QTY	QTY	QTY	QTY	QTY	QTY

Products
Inventory

YEAR:	DATE:					
DESCRIPTION	QTY	QTY	QTY	QTY	QTY	QTY

Products
Inventory

YEAR:	DATE:					
DESCRIPTION	QTY	QTY	QTY	QTY	QTY	QTY

Packaging Materials
Inventory

YEAR:	DATE:					
DESCRIPTION	QTY	QTY	QTY	QTY	QTY	QTY

Marketing Materials
Inventory

DESCRIPTION	QTY	QTY	QTY	QTY	QTY	QTY
YEAR:						
DATE:						

Running Out Of
Tracker

DATE:	PURCHASE BY:
PRODUCT MATERIALS:	**PACKAGING MATERIALS:**

PRODUCT MATERIALS:
- ☐
- ☐
- ☐
- ☐
- ☐
- ☐
- ☐
- ☐
- ☐
- ☐
- ☐
- ☐
- ☐
- ☐
- ☐
- ☐
- ☐
- ☐
- ☐
- ☐
- ☐

PACKAGING MATERIALS:
- ☐
- ☐
- ☐
- ☐
- ☐
- ☐
- ☐
- ☐
- ☐
- ☐
- ☐
- ☐
- ☐
- ☐
- ☐
- ☐
- ☐
- ☐
- ☐
- ☐

Running Out Of
Tracker

DATE:	PURCHASE BY:
PRODUCT MATERIALS:	**PACKAGING MATERIALS:**

☐ ....
☐ ....
☐ ....
☐ ....
☐ ....
☐ ....
☐ ....
☐ ....
☐ ....
☐ ....
☐ ....
☐ ....
☐ ....
☐ ....
☐ ....
☐ ....
☐ ....
☐ ....
☐ ....
☐ ....
☐ ....
☐

Social Media Strategy

INSTAGRAM

ACCOUNT NAME:

POST FREQUENCY:

CONTENT IDEAS:

PURPOSE / GOAL:

PINTEREST

ACCOUNT NAME:

POST FREQUENCY:

CONTENT IDEAS:

PURPOSE / GOAL:

TWITTER

ACCOUNT NAME:

POST FREQUENCY:

CONTENT IDEAS:

PURPOSE / GOAL:

FACEBOOK

ACCOUNT NAME:

POST FREQUENCY:

CONTENT IDEAS:

PURPOSE / GOAL:

OTHER:

ACCOUNT NAME:

POST FREQUENCY:

CONTENT IDEAS:

PURPOSE / GOAL:

OTHER:

ACCOUNT NAME:

POST FREQUENCY:

CONTENT IDEAS:

PURPOSE / GOAL:

NOTES AND OTHER IDEAS:

Social Media Strategy

INSTAGRAM

ACCOUNT NAME:

POST FREQUENCY:

CONTENT IDEAS:

PURPOSE / GOAL:

PINTEREST

ACCOUNT NAME:

POST FREQUENCY:

CONTENT IDEAS:

PURPOSE / GOAL:

TWITTER

ACCOUNT NAME:

POST FREQUENCY:

CONTENT IDEAS:

PURPOSE / GOAL:

FACEBOOK

ACCOUNT NAME:

POST FREQUENCY:

CONTENT IDEAS:

PURPOSE / GOAL:

OTHER:

ACCOUNT NAME:

POST FREQUENCY:

CONTENT IDEAS:

PURPOSE / GOAL:

OTHER:

ACCOUNT NAME:

POST FREQUENCY:

CONTENT IDEAS:

PURPOSE / GOAL:

NOTES AND OTHER IDEAS:

Social Media Strategy

INSTAGRAM

ACCOUNT NAME:

POST FREQUENCY:

CONTENT IDEAS:

PURPOSE / GOAL:

PINTEREST

ACCOUNT NAME:

POST FREQUENCY:

CONTENT IDEAS:

PURPOSE / GOAL:

TWITTER

ACCOUNT NAME:

POST FREQUENCY:

CONTENT IDEAS:

PURPOSE / GOAL:

FACEBOOK

ACCOUNT NAME:

POST FREQUENCY:

CONTENT IDEAS:

PURPOSE / GOAL:

OTHER:

ACCOUNT NAME:

POST FREQUENCY:

CONTENT IDEAS:

PURPOSE / GOAL:

OTHER:

ACCOUNT NAME:

POST FREQUENCY:

CONTENT IDEAS:

PURPOSE / GOAL:

NOTES AND OTHER IDEAS:

Social Media Strategy

INSTAGRAM	PINTEREST
ACCOUNT NAME:	ACCOUNT NAME:
POST FREQUENCY:	POST FREQUENCY:
CONTENT IDEAS:	CONTENT IDEAS:
PURPOSE / GOAL:	PURPOSE / GOAL:

TWITTER	FACEBOOK
ACCOUNT NAME:	ACCOUNT NAME:
POST FREQUENCY:	POST FREQUENCY:
CONTENT IDEAS:	CONTENT IDEAS:
PURPOSE / GOAL:	PURPOSE / GOAL:

OTHER:	OTHER:
ACCOUNT NAME:	ACCOUNT NAME:
POST FREQUENCY:	POST FREQUENCY:
CONTENT IDEAS:	CONTENT IDEAS:
PURPOSE / GOAL:	PURPOSE / GOAL:

NOTES AND OTHER IDEAS:

Social Media Strategy

_____

INSTAGRAM

ACCOUNT NAME:

POST FREQUENCY:

CONTENT IDEAS:

PURPOSE / GOAL:

PINTEREST

ACCOUNT NAME:

POST FREQUENCY:

CONTENT IDEAS:

PURPOSE / GOAL:

TWITTER

ACCOUNT NAME:

POST FREQUENCY:

CONTENT IDEAS:

PURPOSE / GOAL:

FACEBOOK

ACCOUNT NAME:

POST FREQUENCY:

CONTENT IDEAS:

PURPOSE / GOAL:

OTHER:

ACCOUNT NAME:

POST FREQUENCY:

CONTENT IDEAS:

PURPOSE / GOAL:

OTHER:

ACCOUNT NAME:

POST FREQUENCY:

CONTENT IDEAS:

PURPOSE / GOAL:

NOTES AND OTHER IDEAS:

Social Media Strategy

INSTAGRAM

ACCOUNT NAME:

POST FREQUENCY:

CONTENT IDEAS:

PURPOSE / GOAL:

PINTEREST

ACCOUNT NAME:

POST FREQUENCY:

CONTENT IDEAS:

PURPOSE / GOAL:

TWITTER

ACCOUNT NAME:

POST FREQUENCY:

CONTENT IDEAS:

PURPOSE / GOAL:

FACEBOOK

ACCOUNT NAME:

POST FREQUENCY:

CONTENT IDEAS:

PURPOSE / GOAL:

OTHER:

ACCOUNT NAME:

POST FREQUENCY:

CONTENT IDEAS:

PURPOSE / GOAL:

OTHER:

ACCOUNT NAME:

POST FREQUENCY:

CONTENT IDEAS:

PURPOSE / GOAL:

NOTES AND OTHER IDEAS:

Social Media Strategy

INSTAGRAM
ACCOUNT NAME:
POST FREQUENCY:
CONTENT IDEAS:
PURPOSE / GOAL:

PINTEREST
ACCOUNT NAME:
POST FREQUENCY:
CONTENT IDEAS:
PURPOSE / GOAL:

TWITTER
ACCOUNT NAME:
POST FREQUENCY:
CONTENT IDEAS:
PURPOSE / GOAL:

FACEBOOK
ACCOUNT NAME:
POST FREQUENCY:
CONTENT IDEAS:
PURPOSE / GOAL:

OTHER:
ACCOUNT NAME:
POST FREQUENCY:
CONTENT IDEAS:
PURPOSE / GOAL:

OTHER:
ACCOUNT NAME:
POST FREQUENCY:
CONTENT IDEAS:
PURPOSE / GOAL:

NOTES AND OTHER IDEAS:

Social Media Strategy

INSTAGRAM

ACCOUNT NAME:

POST FREQUENCY:

CONTENT IDEAS:

PURPOSE / GOAL:

PINTEREST

ACCOUNT NAME:

POST FREQUENCY:

CONTENT IDEAS:

PURPOSE / GOAL:

TWITTER

ACCOUNT NAME:

POST FREQUENCY:

CONTENT IDEAS:

PURPOSE / GOAL:

FACEBOOK

ACCOUNT NAME:

POST FREQUENCY:

CONTENT IDEAS:

PURPOSE / GOAL:

OTHER:

ACCOUNT NAME:

POST FREQUENCY:

CONTENT IDEAS:

PURPOSE / GOAL:

OTHER:

ACCOUNT NAME:

POST FREQUENCY:

CONTENT IDEAS:

PURPOSE / GOAL:

NOTES AND OTHER IDEAS:

Social Media Strategy

_____

INSTAGRAM

ACCOUNT NAME:

POST FREQUENCY:

CONTENT IDEAS:

PURPOSE / GOAL:

PINTEREST

ACCOUNT NAME:

POST FREQUENCY:

CONTENT IDEAS:

PURPOSE / GOAL:

TWITTER

ACCOUNT NAME:

POST FREQUENCY:

CONTENT IDEAS:

PURPOSE / GOAL:

FACEBOOK

ACCOUNT NAME:

POST FREQUENCY:

CONTENT IDEAS:

PURPOSE / GOAL:

OTHER:

ACCOUNT NAME:

POST FREQUENCY:

CONTENT IDEAS:

PURPOSE / GOAL:

OTHER:

ACCOUNT NAME:

POST FREQUENCY:

CONTENT IDEAS:

PURPOSE / GOAL:

NOTES AND OTHER IDEAS:

Social Media Strategy

INSTAGRAM

ACCOUNT NAME:

POST FREQUENCY:

CONTENT IDEAS:

PURPOSE / GOAL:

PINTEREST

ACCOUNT NAME:

POST FREQUENCY:

CONTENT IDEAS:

PURPOSE / GOAL:

TWITTER

ACCOUNT NAME:

POST FREQUENCY:

CONTENT IDEAS:

PURPOSE / GOAL:

FACEBOOK

ACCOUNT NAME:

POST FREQUENCY:

CONTENT IDEAS:

PURPOSE / GOAL:

OTHER:

ACCOUNT NAME:

POST FREQUENCY:

CONTENT IDEAS:

PURPOSE / GOAL:

OTHER:

ACCOUNT NAME:

POST FREQUENCY:

CONTENT IDEAS:

PURPOSE / GOAL:

NOTES AND OTHER IDEAS:

Marketing Campaign Planner

CAMPAIGN:

DATES:

PURPOSE:

WHERE TO PROMOTE:

GOALS

TO-DO + PREP

- [ ]
- [ ]
- [ ]
- [ ]
- [ ]
- [ ]
- [ ]
- [ ]
- [ ]
- [ ]
- [ ]

SCHEDULE + TIMELINE

DATE	POST
	☐
	☐
	☐
	☐
	☐
	☐
	☐
	☐
	☐
	☐
	☐
	☐

NOTES AND FOLLOW UP IDEAS:

RESULTS

MONEY EARNED:

NEW EMAIL SUBSCRIBERS:

NEW FOLLOWERS:

OTHER:

Marketing Campaign Planner

CAMPAIGN:

DATES:

PURPOSE:

WHERE TO PROMOTE:

GOALS

TO-DO + PREP

☐
☐
☐
☐
☐
☐
☐
☐
☐
☐
☐
☐

SCHEDULE + TIMELINE

DATE	POST	
		☐
		☐
		☐
		☐
		☐
		☐
		☐
		☐
		☐
		☐
		☐
		☐

NOTES AND FOLLOW UP IDEAS:

RESULTS

MONEY EARNED:

NEW EMAIL SUBSCRIBERS:

NEW FOLLOWERS:

OTHER:

Marketing Campaign Planner

CAMPAIGN:

DATES:

PURPOSE:

WHERE TO PROMOTE:

GOALS

TO-DO + PREP

☐
☐
☐
☐
☐
☐
☐
☐
☐
☐
☐
☐

SCHEDULE + TIMELINE

DATE	POST
	☐
	☐
	☐
	☐
	☐
	☐
	☐
	☐
	☐
	☐
	☐
	☐

NOTES AND FOLLOW UP IDEAS:

RESULTS

MONEY EARNED:

NEW EMAIL SUBSCRIBERS:

NEW FOLLOWERS:

OTHER:

Marketing Campaign Planner

CAMPAIGN:

DATES:

PURPOSE:

WHERE TO PROMOTE:

GOALS

TO-DO + PREP

☐
☐
☐
☐
☐
☐
☐
☐
☐
☐
☐
☐
☐

SCHEDULE + TIMELINE

DATE	POST
	☐
	☐
	☐
	☐
	☐
	☐
	☐
	☐
	☐
	☐
	☐
	☐

NOTES AND FOLLOW UP IDEAS:

RESULTS

MONEY EARNED:

NEW EMAIL SUBSCRIBERS:

NEW FOLLOWERS:

OTHER:

Marketing Campaign Planner

CAMPAIGN:

DATES:

PURPOSE:

WHERE TO PROMOTE:

GOALS

TO-DO + PREP

- ☐
- ☐
- ☐
- ☐
- ☐
- ☐
- ☐
- ☐
- ☐
- ☐
- ☐
- ☐

SCHEDULE + TIMELINE

DATE	POST	
		☐
		☐
		☐
		☐
		☐
		☐
		☐
		☐
		☐
		☐
		☐
		☐

NOTES AND FOLLOW UP IDEAS:

RESULTS

MONEY EARNED:

NEW EMAIL SUBSCRIBERS:

NEW FOLLOWERS:

OTHER:

Facebook Ads
Planner

CAMPAIGN NAME:

| TYPE: | *Goals* | FINANCIAL GOAL: | CONVERSIONS: |
| OBJECTIVE: | | REACH GOAL: | SUBSCRIBERS: |

AD SET NAME:

| AD NAME: | AD ID: |

IMAGE(S) / VIDEO DESCRIPTION:	URL:
	DISPLAY LINK:
	HEADLINE:
	TEXT:

NOTES:

Facebook Ads
Planner

CAMPAIGN NAME:

TYPE:	*Goals*	FINANCIAL GOAL:	CONVERSIONS:
OBJECTIVE:		REACH GOAL:	SUBSCRIBERS:

AD SET NAME:

AD NAME:

AD ID:

IMAGE(S) / VIDEO DESCRIPTION:

URL:

DISPLAY LINK:

HEADLINE:

TEXT:

NOTES:

Facebook Ads
Planner

CAMPAIGN NAME:

| TYPE: | *Goals* | FINANCIAL GOAL: | CONVERSIONS: |
| OBJECTIVE: | | REACH GOAL: | SUBSCRIBERS: |

AD SET NAME:

AD NAME:

AD ID:

IMAGE(S) / VIDEO DESCRIPTION:

URL:

DISPLAY LINK:

HEADLINE:

TEXT:

NOTES:

Facebook Ads
Tracker

DATE	AD NAME	DELIVERY	RESULTS	REACH	IMPRESSIONS	COST PER RESULT	BUDGET	AMOUNT SPENT	ENDS

Facebook Ads
Tracker

DATE	AD NAME	DELIVERY	RESULTS	REACH	IMPRESSIONS	COST PER RESULT	BUDGET	AMOUNT SPENT	ENDS

Facebook Ads
Tracker

DATE	AD NAME	DELIVERY	RESULTS	REACH	IMPRESSIONS	COST PER RESULT	BUDGET	AMOUNT SPENT	ENDS

Reach Stats
Yearly Overview

YEAR:					
	NEWSLETTER	INSTAGRAM	PINTEREST	FACEBOOK	TWITTER
J					
F					
M					
A					
M					
J					
J					
A					
S					
O					
N					
D					

Reach Stats
Yearly Overview

YEAR:					
	NEWSLETTER	INSTAGRAM	PINTEREST	FACEBOOK	TWITTER
J					
F					
M					
A					
M					
J					
J					
A					
S					
O					
N					
D					

Reach Stats
Yearly Overview

YEAR:					
	NEWSLETTER	INSTAGRAM	PINTEREST	FACEBOOK	TWITTER
J					
F					
M					
A					
M					
J					
J					
A					
S					
O					
N					
D					

Boutique's Analytics
Yearly Overview

YEAR:						
	VISITS	ORDERS	REVENUE	BEST SELLER	MAIN TRAFFIC SOURCE	MOST VISITED PRODUCT
J						
F						
M						
A						
M						
J						
J						
A						
S						
O						
N						
D						

Monthly Income
Tracker

DATE	DESCRIPTION	ORDER NO.	TOTAL
		TOTAL:	

Monthly Outcome
Tracker

_____

DATE	DESCRIPTION	TAXES / VAT	TOTAL
		TOTAL:	

Monthly Recurring Expenses
Tracker

DATE	DESCRIPTION	VAT/TAXES	TOTAL
		TOTAL:	

Yearly Progress Overview

YEAR:					

	INCOME	OUTCOME	PROFIT		
J					
F					
M					
A					
M					
J					
J					
A					
S					
O					
N					
D					
TOTAL:					

10K
9K
8K
7K
6K
5K
4K
3K
2K
1K

J F M A M J J A S O N D

Yearly Finances in Review

_____

HOW DO I FEEL ABOUT THIS YEAR'S GROWTH/DECLINE IN MY INCOME?

WHAT WORKED WELL?	WHAT DIDN'T WORK WELL?	WHAT CAN I IMPROVE?

HOW DO I FEEL ABOUT THIS YEAR'S GROWTH/DECLINE IN MY OUTCOME?

WHAT WORKED WELL?	WHAT DIDN'T WORK WELL?	WHAT CAN I IMPROVE?

NOTES AND OTHER IDEAS:

Boutique's Tasks
Overview

DAILY TASKS
☐
☐
☐
☐
☐
☐
☐
☐
☐
☐

WEEKLY TASKS
☐
☐
☐
☐
☐
☐
☐
☐
☐
☐

MONTHLY TASKS
☐
☐
☐
☐
☐

QUARTERLY TASKS
☐
☐
☐
☐
☐

YEARLY TASKS
☐
☐
☐
☐
☐

NOTES:

Boutique's Monthly
Planner

_____

MONTH:

M	T	W	Th	F	S	Su

NOTES:	NEXT MONTH:

Boutique's Weekly
Planner

_____

WEEK:

M	
T	
W	
Th	
F	
S	
Su	

WEEKLY GOALS

1: ☐

2: ☐

3: ☐

TASKS

☐
☐
☐
☐
☐
☐
☐
☐
☐
☐

PROMOTIONS / COUPON CODES:

NOTES FOR NEXT WEEK:

To-Do Lists

DATE:

TO-DO LIST FOR:	TO-DO LIST FOR:
☐	☐
☐	☐
☐	☐
☐	☐
☐	☐
☐	☐
☐	☐
☐	☐
☐	☐
☐	☐
☐	☐
☐	☐
☐	☐
☐	☐
☐	☐
☐	☐
☐	☐
☐	☐
☐	☐
☐	☐

My Contacts
Master List

VENDOR	PRODUCT	CONTACT INFO
Dear Lover		

Vendors
Contact Master List

VENDOR	PRODUCT	CONTACT INFO

My Passwords

WEBSITE	EMAIL USED	USERNAME	PASSWORD

Notes

DATE:

Notes

DATE:

Notes

DATE:

Notes

DATE:

Notes

DATE:

"Do one thing you think you cannot do.
Fail at it. Try again.
Do better the second time.
The only people who never tumble
are those who never mount the high wire.
This is your moment. Own it."

Oprah Winfrey

Thank You Beautiful!

HOPE YOU ENJOYED USING YOUR BOUTIQUE PLANNER!

BY THE WAY, I HAVE A FREE BOUTIQUE MINI COURSE TRAINING JUST FOR YOU.

HEAD ON OVER TO WWW.BOUTIQUEVIPLIST.COM TO WATCH IT.

COME JOIN MY PRIVATE GROUP ON FACEBOOK AND NETWORK WITH OTHER ENTREPRENEURIAL MINDED WOMEN

WWW.RICHGIRLCOLLECTIVE.COM

61856867R00077

Made in the USA
Middletown, DE
16 January 2018